22 Effective Dental Marketing Strategies:

Propel Your Clinic to Success with Artificial Intelligence

Claudio Montes

ISBN: 9798883865236

Wellcome

My name is Claudio Montes, and it is my pleasure to welcome you to this book dedicated to exploring effective dental marketing strategies. I am a graphic designer by profession with over 20 years of experience in the digital world and website development. I have had the privilege of participating in the transformation and evolution of traditional media and businesses in general towards the online world over these years.

My journey in the Internet realm has led me to specialize in a particularly exciting and challenging field: digital marketing, especially focused on dental clinics. For over four years, I have been devoted to understanding the complexities and unique opportunities that this specific niche offers. I have worked with dental clinics of all types and sizes, from small offices to clinics with branches in different cities.

Throughout this experience, I have learned the importance of adapting effective strategies to the unique needs and challenges of dental clinics. That's why I have dedicated these years to perfecting these strategies, and now I want to share that knowledge with you.

This book is designed to serve as a comprehensive guide that will help you navigate the exciting world of dental marketing.

Allow me to share with you the strategies and knowledge that will help propel your dental clinic to success.

Table of Contents

Introduction

Welcome to my book on effective Dental Marketing Strategies. This book is a comprehensive guide designed to help you excel in the competitive world of dental care, using proven marketing strategies, and, most excitingly, artificial intelligence (AI).

Dentistry is a noble profession, focused on improving people's health and quality of life, but it is also a highly competitive field. Whether you lead an independent dental clinic or are part of a larger network, the success of this practice depends largely on the ability to attract, retain, and build loyalty with new patients. In a constantly changing digital world, mastering marketing techniques is essential to stand out and thrive.

The good news is that dental marketing has evolved significantly in recent years. In the era of information and technology, opportunities to promote your clinic and reach new patients are more accessible than ever. And, in this book, we will explore an additional element that has revolutionized dental marketing: Artificial Intelligence.

Artificial intelligence is not only transforming healthcare in general but also making a significant impact on the dental industry. From personalizing marketing campaigns to automating administrative tasks, AI is changing how dental professionals connect with patients and manage their practices. As we progress through this book, you will see how you can harness AI to propel your clinic to success.

Before delving into marketing strategies and AI, I want to share a story with you. Imagine a young dentist who has just opened his own dental clinic. He is excited and passionate about his work, but he also realizes that he faces significant challenges. The competition is fierce, and he has a limited marketing budget. Over time, the young dentist realizes that he needs more than just exceptional clinical skills for his clinic to thrive. He needs strategies.

This book is a response to that need. Throughout these pages, I will take you on a journey through 22 effective dental marketing strategies, designed to attract new patients, retain existing ones, and build a strong brand for your dental clinic. Whether you are a newcomer to the marketing world or someone who has already ventured into marketing initiatives, you will find practical advice and innovative strategies that you can apply to achieve tangible results.

Why Dental Marketing?

You might be wondering why dental marketing is so crucial in the first place. After all, shouldn't providing excellent service and dental care be enough? While the quality of care is undoubtedly a determining factor for long-term success, marketing is the key to getting patients through your door in the first place. When you open a dental clinic or center, no one will come to your practice if no one knows you're there.

In these times of digital and computational revolution and expansion, most people seek medical services online before making important healthcare decisions. This includes finding a dentist. If your clinic is not online or lacks a compelling digital presence, potential patients are likely not to find you. Effective dental marketing helps you become visible and appealing to these potential patients.

Moreover, marketing is not just about attracting new patients; it's also about retaining existing patients and fostering lasting relationships with them. Dental marketing provides you with the tools to communicate with your patients, educate them about the importance of ongoing dental care, and keep them engaged with your clinic.

The power of Artificial Intelligence

As we progress through the book, we will also explore one of the most exciting and disruptive trends in dental marketing: Artificial Intelligence (AI). AI is transforming how dental clinics interact with patients and manage their daily operations. From chatbots capable of answering patients' most frequent questions to advanced analytics tools that help optimize marketing strategies, AI is opening new opportunities to enhance efficiency and effectiveness in the dental world.

AI also allows for deeper personalization in marketing strategies. With data analysis and machine learning, you can tailor your messages and offers to meet the specific needs of each patient. This not only increases the effectiveness of your campaigns but also creates a more engaging and relevant experience for your patients. One of the most widely used Artificial Intelligence tools, and one we will utilize throughout this book, is Chat GPT.

What is Chat GPT?

In the current digital era, technology is advancing by leaps and bounds, and with it, innovations emerge that transform the way we conduct business, communicate, and provide healthcare services, including dentistry. One of these innovations that has revolutionized the world of communication and marketing is artificial intelligence, and specifically, GPT-3, a natural language processing model created by OpenAI.

The rise of Chat GPT

GPT-3, or Generative Pre-trained Transformer 3, is one of the most remarkable creations in the field of artificial intelligence. Developed by OpenAI, GPT-3 is a language model trained on an extensive amount of textual data from the internet, enabling it to comprehend and generate text in a surprisingly coherent and contextual manner. Chat GPT is a specific application of this model that facilitates conversation and natural language text generation.

The history of GPT-3 and its evolution is grounded in decades of research in the field of artificial intelligence. As algorithms and natural language processing capabilities have improved, GPT-3 has emerged as one of the most advanced and versatile creations in its category. Its ability to understand context, answer questions, and generate coherent text has sparked significant interest across various industries.

The Chat GPT Revolution

The true revolution of Chat GPT lies in its ability to interact almost humanly with people. As artificial intelligence becomes integrated into more aspects of our lives, from virtual assistants to website chatbots, Chat GPT stands out as a versatile tool that can transform the way businesses engage with their customers and patients.

In the field of dentistry and healthcare at large, Chat GPT is redefining the generation of relevant content and communication with patients through quick, smooth, and coherent responses, as well as scheduling appointments 24/7.

Chat GPT in the World of Dental Clinics

So, how can Chat GPT help increase a dental clinic's patient base? The answer lies in its ability to enhance the patient experience and provide exceptional service. Here are some ways in which Chat GPT can be invaluable for your dental clinic:

1. 24/7 customer support

Chat GPT is available 24 hours a day, 7 days a week. This means that patients can get answers to their questions at any time, even outside the clinic's regular hours. This demonstrates a commitment to service and patient convenience.

2. Fast and Accurate Responses

Chat GPT is designed to understand and respond to questions accurately and efficiently. It can provide information about dental services, insurance, procedures, and more, aiding patients in making informed decisions.

3. Simplified Appointment Scheduling

Chat GPT can integrate with online appointment scheduling systems, making it easy for patients to schedule appointments without having to call or email. This enhances efficiency and accessibility.

4. Education and Commitment

You can use Chat GPT to provide patients with dental care tips, information about procedures, and appointment reminders. This not only educates patients but also encourages greater engagement in their oral health.

5. Help with Marketing Strategies

Chat GPT can significantly contribute to the marketing strategies of your dental clinic and assist in converting visitors into patients. This enhances the effectiveness of your online presence and has the potential to increase the conversion of visitors into patients.

The future of Dentistry with Chat GPT

As artificial intelligence continues to evolve, the role of Chat GPT in dental marketing and care will continue to grow. Chat GPT's ability to adapt and learn from interactions with patients means it can further personalize responses and provide an even more exceptional service over time.

In this book, we will explore how you can effectively integrate Chat GPT into your dental clinic to enhance communication, increase patient satisfaction, boost effective marketing strategies, and expand your clinic's patient base. As we navigate through this exciting era of technology, Chat GPT stands as a valuable ally in the success of your dental clinic.

Chat GPT

To start interacting with Chat GPT, you should go to the following site and create an account at:

https://chat.openai.com/

I recommend that you create different Chats, depending on what you want to ask, as each chat will serve as context for continuing to ask questions based on the same topic. The questions or instructions given to Chat GPT are technically known as prompts or commands. To make Chat GPT's responses more precise, you can instruct it to take on a specific role.

For example:

"Act as an expert content writer and create a Facebook post about proper teeth brushing."

You can also provide more context to your questions, and the responses you receive will be more accurate to the reality of your clinic.

For example:

"I am the owner of a dental clinic in a commercial neighborhood in Santiago, Chile. My primary patients are office workers aged 30 to 45 who work in the area, and my main treatments are teeth whitening and root canals. Give me 3 ideas on how to increase my patients through Instagram."

Now, let's begin with the strategies.

1. Website Optimization

In the digital age, an effective website is one of the most valuable tools for any dental clinic. Your website is often the first impression potential patients have of your service, and it can also be a continuous source of patients and referrals.

The Importance of an Optimized Website

Imagine a potential patient searching for a dentist online. What if their website doesn't appear in the search results? Or worse yet, what if the website is difficult to navigate, slow to load, or not mobile-friendly? In many cases, the patient will simply move on to the next option in the search list. That's why website optimization is essential.

Make it Easy for Patients to Find you

Search Engine Optimization, or SEO, is a key practice to ensure that your website is visible on search engines like Google. When your website ranks well in search results, it increases the likelihood that potential patients will find you when searching for dental services in your area.

User Experience

An optimized website is not just about being visible; it's also about providing an excellent user experience. Patients want to find the information they need quickly and easily. If your website is easy to navigate, loads quickly, and has design for mobile devices, you're one step closer to converting visitors into new patients.

Build Credibility

A professional and well-organized website creates a sense of credibility and trust with potential patients. When visitors encounter a well-built and up-to-date website, they are more likely to trust your dental clinic and feel comfortable scheduling an appointment.

Keys to Optimize your Dental Website

Now that we have established the importance of website optimization, it's time to explore how to do it effectively. Here are some key essentials to ensure that your website is in its best shape:

1. Attractive and Professional Design

An attractive and professional design is the first impression visitors will have of your dental clinic. Ensure that your site's design is clean, organized, and representative of your brand. Colors, fonts, and images should be consistent with your clinic's identity.

2. Relevant and Quality Content

The content of your website is crucial. It should be informative and relevant to patients. This includes descriptions of your services, team biographies, contact information, and educational content about oral health. Additionally, regularly update your blog or news section with helpful articles.

3. Optimization for Mobile Devices

With an increasing number of people accessing the internet from mobile devices, it is crucial that your website is compatible with smartphones and tablets. A responsive design ensures that your site looks and functions well on all screens.

4. Loading Speed

The website loading speed is essential. Slow websites can lead to a high bounce rate, meaning visitors leave your site before any interaction. Optimize images and use an efficient code structure to speed up the loading time.

5. Local SEO

If you want to attract local patients, local SEO is key. Make sure to include accurate location information on your website and verify your profile on Google My Business to enhance your local visibility. I will explain this in more detail in a later chapter.

6. Ease of Navigation

Navigation should be intuitive. Visitors should be able to find information easily. Use a logical menu structure and place strategic calls to action (CTAs) to guide visitors to take actions, such as scheduling an appointment.

7. Security and SSL Certificate

Security is essential on a healthcare website and instills confidence when entering a site. Ensure you have an SSL certificate installed to protect patient information and boost trust in your site. To check if a website has an SSL certificate, browsers display a padlock icon before the URL, indicating that it is a secure site.

Tools for Optimizing your Website

With some free tools, you can visualize how your visitors interact, the most visited sections, and the time users spend on your website.

Google Page Speed

https://pagespeed.web.dev/

This free Google tool is used to obtain a website loading speed report and optimization tips.

Google Analytics

https://analytics.google.com/

With Google Analytics, you can see the number of real-time visitors, the most visited pages, user interaction time, as well as a myriad of reports and tools.

HotJar

https://www.hotjar.com

This tool can record all website visitors to observe how users interact and which sections they spend more time on (heatmap).

Chat GPT Prompt Ideas to get Suggestions on How to Optimize your Website

Some commands or prompts you can use in Chat GPT to optimize your dental clinic website include:

"Can you suggest ways to improve the loading speed of my dental clinic website?"

"What local SEO strategies are most effective for a dental clinic?"

"How can I structure the navigation menu of my dental clinic website to make it more intuitive?"

"What type of content is most effective in attracting new patients to my dental clinic?"

"What are the best practices to keep my website secure and protected?"

In summary, optimizing your dental website is essential to attract and retain patients in the digital age. Combine best practices in design and content with artificial intelligence to create an effective website that not only attracts visitors but converts them into satisfied patients.

2. Social Networks Marketing

In the digital age, social media has become an essential tool for business promotion, including dental clinics. Platforms like Facebook and Instagram offer unique opportunities to connect with your patients, showcase your expertise, and build strong relationships with your audience. In this section, we will explore how to effectively use social media marketing to propel your dental clinic towards success.

The Impact of Social Networks on Dental Health

Social media has transformed the way people access information and communicate with each other. In the context of dental care, this means that patients not only seek recommendations from friends and family but also research and evaluate dental clinics online before making a decision. This makes social media an invaluable tool for promoting your dental clinic.

Connection with the Community

Social media allows you to connect directly with your local community and beyond. You can engage with current and potential patients, answer questions, share news, and create a sense of online community around your dental clinic.

Visibility and Brand Recognition

Social media marketing is an effective way to increase the visibility of your dental clinic. Posting content regularly on popular platforms like Facebook and Instagram helps you create brand awareness and establish a strong online presence.

Education and Awareness

Social media is an effective channel to educate your audience about the importance of dental health. You can share dental care tips, information about procedures, and oral health news to help your followers make informed decisions about their dental care.

Effective Marketing Strategies in Social Networks

Now that you understand why social media marketing is important, let's explore some effective strategies to make the most of these platforms:

1. Identify your Audience

Before you start, it's crucial to identify who you're targeting on social media. Are they primarily families, young adults, or a specific demographic group? Knowing your audience will help you tailor your content and the tone of your posts effectively.

2. Create a Content Calendar

Plan your content in advance. Create a posting calendar that includes relevant topics such as dental care tips, patient success stories, and special promotions. Consistency in posting is key to keeping your audience engaged.

3. Publish a Variety of Content

Diversify your content to keep it interesting and relevant. Post pictures of your team, patient testimonials, educational videos, and dental industry news. Diversity in content will attract a broader audience.

4. Interact with your Audience

Don't limit yourself to posting content; interact with your followers. Respond to questions and comments promptly and friendly. Genuine interaction builds strong online relationships.

5. Promote Special Offers

Social media is an effective channel to promote special offers and discounts on your dental services. Advertise exclusive promotions for your social media followers to encourage engagement.

6. Use Paid Advertising

Consider the possibility of investing in paid advertising on social media to reach a broader and targeted audience. Targeting options allow you to reach specific individuals based on location, interests, and more.

Chat GPT Prompt Ideas to Create and Publish Articles of Interest and Dental Health

Using artificial intelligence to create and publish content on social media can be an effective strategy. Some prompt or command ideas for Chat GPT include:

"Generate an article on the importance of regular teeth brushing and how to choose the best toothpaste."

"Write a post on how to maintain a healthy smile in summer, including tips on diet and dental care."

"Create an informative post about the benefits of invisible braces for adults."

"Write a short article on how to avoid and treat tooth sensitivity."

"Generate a fun and educational post about the relationship between oral health and overall health."

You can accompany your post with an image or stock photograph. There are sites where you can search for and use royalty-free photos, such as https://www.pexels.com or https://www.freepik.com.

In summary, social media marketing is a powerful tool to promote your dental clinic and build relationships with patients. Take advantage of these platforms to connect with your community, educate your audience, and increase the visibility of your clinic.

3. Loyalty and Referral Programs

In the ongoing pursuit of sustainable and successful growth for your dental clinic, it is essential not only to attract new patients but also to keep current patients happy and encourage them to share their positive experiences with friends and family. Loyalty and referral programs are powerful tools that can strengthen patient relationships and increase your clinic's patient base. In this section, we will explore the importance of these programs and how to implement them effectively.

The Importance of Patient Loyalty

Before delving into the details of loyalty and referral programs, it's important to understand why patient loyalty is fundamental to the success of your dental clinic.

Patient Retention

Retaining existing patients is more cost-effective than acquiring new ones. Loyal patients are more likely to return for future treatments and services, increasing profitability over time.

Relationship Building

Patient loyalty is not just about transactions; it's about building strong relationships with your patients. When patients feel valued and well-cared for, they are more likely to become advocates for your clinic and recommend your services to family and friends.

Marketing cost Reduction

The cost of acquiring new patients through marketing strategies can be significant. By fostering patient loyalty, you reduce the reliance on acquiring new patients through advertising.

Creating Effective Loyalty Programs

Now that we understand the importance of patient loyalty, let's explore how to create effective loyalty programs for your dental clinic.

1. Identify your best Patients

Start by identifying your most loyal and valuable patients. These may be individuals who have been receiving treatment at your clinic for years or those who have referred other patients. Recognizing and rewarding these patients is an important step.

2. Offer Relevant Incentives

The incentives should be relevant to your patients. They can include discounts on future treatments, gifts, free services, or even loyalty program memberships.

3. Clear Communication

Ensure that your patients are aware of the loyalty program and how they can participate. Clearly communicate the benefits through your website, social media, and in the clinic.

4. Tracking and Recognition

Keep track of interactions and the behavior of your loyal patients. Acknowledge their loyalty regularly and in a personalized manner, whether through thank-you notes, calls, or special messages on their birthdays.

5. Ask for Feedback

Ask your loyal patients to share their opinions and suggestions to improve your clinic. Their feedback can be invaluable for making adjustments and providing better service.

Referral Programs

Referral programs are a natural extension of loyalty programs and can be a powerful way to attract new patients through recommendations from your existing patients.

1. Rewards for Referrals

Offer incentives for both the referred patient and the referrer. For instance, you could provide a treatment discount for the referred patient and a thank-you bonus for the referrer.

2. Makes Reference Easy

Simplify the referral process for your patients. Provide referral cards they can share with friends and family, or establish an online system where they can easily submit referrals.

3. Highlight Success Stories

Share success stories of referred patients on your website and social media. This not only showcases the value of your services but also acknowledges and thanks patients for their referrals.

Ideas for Chat GPT Prompts to Request Suggestions and Advice for Loyalty and Referrals

If you're seeking specific suggestions and tips for customer loyalty and creating effective referral programs in your dental clinic, you can use artificial intelligence for ideas.

Here are some prompt ideas for Chat GPT:

"Provide tips to keep patients engaged and loyal to my dental clinic."

"Generate ideas for effective incentives I can offer to encourage patients to recommend my dental clinic to friends and family."

"What are the best practices for automating communication with patients and reminding them of their dental appointments?"

"What strategies can I use to identify patients most likely to refer

others?"

"Give me suggestions for highlighting success stories of referred patients in my social media marketing."

In summary, loyalty and referral programs are valuable tools to strengthen patient relationships and attract new ones. Seize the opportunity to recognize and reward your patients' loyalty while encouraging word-of-mouth recommendations. Artificial intelligence can help enhance the effectiveness of these strategies and provide exceptional service to your patients.

4. Local Online Presence (Local SEO)

Local online presence is an essential component of dental marketing in the digital era. As patients search for healthcare services, including dental services, online, it's crucial that your dental clinic is easily accessible and well-represented in local online directories. In this section, we will explore the importance of local online presence and how to ensure that your dental clinic is in the spotlight for local patients.

The Importance of Local Presence

Local online presence refers to how your dental clinic is showcased on the web in close relation to the physical location of your clinic. This includes appearing in local directories and search engines when patients search for dental services in your area. The importance of local presence lies in several key factors:

Visibility for Local Patients

When patients search for a dentist online, they are likely to use search terms that include location, such as "dentist in [city]" or "dental clinic near me," or even conduct searches on Google Maps or any other map-based search engine. Having a strong local presence ensures that your clinic appears in the search results for these patients.

Credibility and Trust

Being present in online local directories, such as Google My Business (currently Google Business Profile), adds a level of credibility and trust to your clinic. Patients can see detailed information about your practice, including reviews from other patients, which can influence their decision to schedule an appointment.

Make it Easy to Contact

Accurate and easily accessible contact information is essential for patients to find and get in touch with you. Local online presence ensures that patients have access to your address, phone number, and office hours.

Maximizing your Local Online Presence

Here are some key strategies to maximize your local online presence:

1. Google My Business (currently Google Business Profile)

Google Business Profile is a powerful tool to increase local visibility. Ensure that your Business Profile account is complete and updated with accurate information, including your address, phone number, and business hours. Post high-quality photos and respond to patient reviews professionally.

2. Local Health Services Directories

Research and register on online health services directories. These industry-specific directories for the medical sector can help you reach patients searching for dental services in your area. Make sure to keep your information up-to-date on these directories.

3. Local Keyword Optimization

Use local keywords in the content of your website and in your Business Profile account. This will increase the chances of appearing in search results when local patients search for dental services.

4. Ask for Reviews from Satisfied Patients

Positive reviews are an important factor in attracting local patients. Encourage your satisfied patients to leave reviews on your Business Profile account and on other relevant directories.

5. Promote Local Events and Offers

If you participate in local events or offer special promotions for local patients, make sure to promote them online. This can attract patients looking for deals and services nearby.

Prompt Ideas to Increase your Local Presence

If you are looking for specific ways to enhance the local presence of your dental clinic on Google Business Profile and local online directories for medical services, you can use artificial intelligence to obtain ideas and advice. Here are some prompt ideas for Chat GPT:

"Generate ideas to optimize the Google My Business profile of my dental clinic and attract more local patients."

"Provide advice on effectively requesting and managing patient reviews online."

"How can I stand out in local health directories online and appear at the top of search results?"

"Give me suggestions for promoting local events on the Google My Business profile of my dental clinic and on my website."

"How can I use local keywords effectively to attract patients from my area in need of dental treatments?"

In summary, local online presence is essential for attracting patients to your dental clinic. Take advantage of these tools and health directories to ensure that your clinic is easily visible to patients seeking dental services in your area.

5. Oral Health Events and Seminars

Organizing dental health events and seminars is an effective strategy to connect with the local community, establish your expertise as a dental professional, and attract potential patients to your clinic. In this section, we will explore the importance of conducting free educational events on dental health in various locations, such as businesses, schools, or childcare centers. You will discover how to plan, promote, and successfully execute these events, which can make a difference in the growth of your dental clinic.

Benefits of Organizing Oral Health Events

Before delving into the planning and execution of oral health events, it is crucial to understand why they are so valuable for your dental clinic.

1. Connection with the Local Community

Events provide you with the opportunity to connect directly with the local community. You can establish personal relationships with attendees and demonstrate your commitment to community oral health.

2. Preventive Education

Educational events allow you to share knowledge about preventive dental care. You can inform the community about the importance of brushing, flossing, and other essential aspects of oral health.

3. Trust Generation

When you provide valuable information for free, you build trust in your expertise and professionalism. Attendees will see that you care about their oral health and will be more inclined to consider you as their trusted dentist.

4. Potential Patients

Events are an opportunity to attract potential patients. Those who attend may be seeking a new dentist or could recommend you to friends and family in the future.

Oral Health Event Planning

To host successful oral health events, follow these steps:

1. Clear Objectives

Clearly define the objectives of your event. Do you want to educate about the importance of oral health in local schools or attract workers from nearby businesses? Having clear goals will help you design the event effectively.

2. Selection of Place and Date

Choose a suitable venue for your event, such as a school, a local business, or a kindergarten. The date should be convenient for your target audience.

3. Educational Content

Plan the content of your presentation or seminar. Consider topics such as cavity prevention, the importance of regular dental visits, and oral care tips. Prepare visual materials and practical examples.

4. Promotion

Promote your event through social media, community flyers, and emails to your current patients. Use multiple channels to reach a broader audience.

5. Resources and Materials

Make sure you have all the necessary resources and materials for the event, such as informative brochures, samples of dental products, and presentation materials.

6. Trained Staff

If possible, have the assistance of trained staff from your dental clinic to answer questions and provide personalized advice to attendees.

Events Promotion on Social Networks

A crucial part of promoting your oral health events is utilizing social media. Here are some ideas on how to promote your events on platforms like Facebook, Instagram, and Twitter:

1. Advertisement Posts

Create promotional posts that highlight the benefits of the event and its educational nature. Use engaging images and colors related to oral health to capture attention.

2. Informative Videos

Record short videos explaining the purpose of the event and what attendees can expect. Post these videos on your social profiles and promote them with paid ads to reach a wider audience.

3. Relevant Hashtags

Use hashtags related to oral health and the event in your posts. This will make it easier for people interested in this topic to find your content.

4. Collaborations with Local Influencers

If possible, collaborate with local influencers related to health or wellness to promote the event. Their followers may be interested in attending.

5. Reminder Posts

Make periodic reminder posts in the days leading up to the event to ensure that people have it on their agenda.

Prompt Ideas to Promote Events on Social Networks

To request Chat GPT's assistance in drafting texts inviting social media followers to participate in an oral health event, you can use prompts such as:

"Generate a Facebook message inviting our followers to our upcoming oral health event at [school or institution name]."

"Help craft an Instagram post highlighting the benefits of attending our oral health event for parents and children, and provide suggestions for which photo to accompany the post."

"Create a Facebook reminder post about our upcoming oral health seminar next week."

"Write a Twitter post emphasizing our dental team's expertise and the importance of dental prevention to encourage attendance at our free event."

In summary, organizing oral health events and seminars is an effective strategy to connect with the community, educate potential patients, and establish your expertise as a dental professional. Social media promotion plays a crucial role in spreading awareness of these events, and you can use Chat GPT to help you craft engaging and persuasive messages that invite followers to participate in your oral health events. With proper planning and an effective promotion strategy, these events can significantly contribute to the growth of your dental clinic.

6. Content Marketing for Dental Clinics

In the digital age, content marketing has become a fundamental tool for dental clinics aiming to establish their online presence, position their expertise, and attract an audience interested in oral health. In this strategy, we will explore how creating a blog on your website and publishing high-quality content on dental topics can be an effective strategy to strengthen your reputation, attract organic traffic, and educate your patients about the importance of preventing oral diseases.

The Importance of Content Marketing

Content marketing goes beyond traditional advertising strategies. It's about providing valuable and relevant information that addresses the questions and needs of your audience. In the case of dental clinics, this strategy can generate a series of benefits:

1. Positioning as Authority

By creating high-quality content on dental topics, you demonstrate your knowledge and expertise in the field. This positions you as a trusted authority in the minds of your patients and potential clients.

2. Attracting Organic Traffic

Quality content attracts organic traffic (unpaid traffic) to your website. When people search for information about oral health, they are more likely to find your site if you have published relevant and search engine-optimized (SEO) content.

3. Patient Education

Content marketing provides you with the opportunity to educate your patients about the importance of dental care and the prevention of oral diseases. You can address topics such as proper brushing, flossing, diet, and other aspects related to oral health.

4. Building Relationships

Quality content can foster strong relationships with your patients. You can answer their questions, provide helpful advice, and keep them engaged between clinic visits.

Creating an effective Dental Blog

Here are the key steps to create and manage an effective dental blog:

1. Identification of Relevant Topics

Research the most relevant and popular topics in the field of dental health. This may include subjects such as cavity prevention, teeth whitening, orthodontics, and other related aspects.

2. Post Scheduling

Establish a regular posting schedule to maintain consistency on your blog. This can be weekly, bi-weekly, or monthly, depending on your resources and availability.

3. SEO Optimization

Ensure that each post is optimized for search engines. Use relevant keywords, meta descriptions, and appropriate headings to increase visibility in search results.

4. Multimedia Content

Enrich your posts with multimedia content such as images, infographics, and videos. This makes the content more engaging and easy to comprehend.

5. Interaction with Readers

Encourage interaction with your readers through comment sections and contact forms. Respond to questions and comments promptly and in a friendly manner.

6. Promotion on Social Networks

Share your blog posts on your social media profiles to increase their reach. You can use platforms like Facebook, Twitter, and Instagram to promote your content.

Chat GPT Prompt Ideas for Creating Educational Content

Educational content creation is crucial for a successful dental blog. You can use Chat GPT to help you draft informative and educational texts about oral health. Here are some prompt ideas to request Chat GPT to generate content:

"Write an educational article on the importance of dental prevention and how patients can maintain healthy smiles."

"Create an article that explains the effects of poor oral health on overall health and how to prevent dental problems."

"Write a step-by-step guide on how to properly care for teeth and gums, including flossing and mouthwash use."

"Generate an article on the benefits of teeth whitening and the different methods available for patients."

In conclusion, content marketing through a dental blog is an effective strategy to establish your online presence, educate your patients, and attract organic traffic. Seize the opportunity to share your expertise and advice on oral health, and use Chat GPT to generate informative and educational content that keeps your audience engaged and well-informed. With a solid content marketing strategy, you can strengthen relationships with your patients, attract new ones, and promote oral health in your community.

7. Online Advertising for Dental Clinics

In the competitive world of dentistry, online advertising has become an essential tool to reach a wider audience and attract new patients. In this section, we will explore the importance of using paid ads on Google Ads and social media to promote your dental clinic. You will learn how to target relevant keywords and use demographic targeting to maximize the effectiveness of your ads and attract those seeking dental services.

The Power of Online Advertising

Online advertising has revolutionized the way dental clinics can reach their audience. Unlike traditional advertising methods, online advertising allows for greater precision in targeting and more effective measurement of return on investment.

Advantages of Online Advertising

Precise targeting: You can direct your ads to specific individuals based on their interests, geographical location, and online behaviors.

Detailed measurement: Obtain accurate data on your ad performance, including the number of clicks, conversions, and cost per acquisition.

Flexibility and control: You have complete control over your budget and the ability to adjust your ads in real-time based on their performance.

Global reach: You can reach a local audience or expand your reach locally or internationally, depending on your objectives.

Using Google Ads for Dental Clinics

Google Ads is one of the most effective online advertising platforms for dental clinics. It allows your ads to appear in Google search results when people are searching for dental services. Here are key steps to leverage Google Ads:

1. Keyword Research

Conduct thorough research on relevant keywords for your dental clinic. Identify keywords that people commonly search for when looking for dental services, such as "dentist in [your location]" or "orthodontic treatment."

2. Campaign Settings

Create specific advertising campaigns and set your daily budget. Use relevant keywords in your ads and create multiple ad groups to target specific audiences.

3. Geographic Segmentation

Use geographical targeting to display your ads only to people within your service area. This ensures that your ads reach individuals who can easily visit your clinic.

4. Monitoring and Optimization

Continuously monitor the performance of your ads on Google Ads. Adjust your keyword strategies and budget based on the results obtained.

Advertising on Social Networks

Social media also offers significant opportunities to promote your dental clinic. Platforms like Facebook, Instagram, and Twitter allow you to reach a broad and highly segmented audience. Here are tips for effective social media advertising:

1. Identification of Target Audience

Clearly define who your ideal patients are. Are you looking to attract families, teenagers, or older adults? Use demographic targeting on social media to reach your target audience.

2. Engaging Visual Content

Use engaging images and videos that showcase the welcoming atmosphere of your dental clinic and the professional team. Before-and-after treatment images are also effective.

3. Special Promotions

Provide special promotions through your social media ads. This can include discounts on routine dental treatments or complimentary additional services.

4. Interaction with the Audience

Encourage interaction with your audience through comments and direct messages. Respond to questions and comments in a friendly and professional manner.

Chat GPT Prompt Ideas for Google Ads

To request Chat GPT's assistance in drafting effective Google Ads that capture the attention of your target audience, you can use prompts such as:

"Generate a Google Ads ad to promote our cosmetic dentistry services and highlight how we can enhance our patients' smiles."

"Write a Google Ads ad that showcases our state-of-the-art dental clinic and the cutting-edge technology we use in our treatments."

"Create a Facebook ad offering a free dental consultation as a special offer for new patients."

"Generate a Google Ads ad promoting our pediatric dental care services and emphasizing our kid-friendly approach."

"Write a persuasive Facebook ad highlighting our expertise in dental implants and how they can restore the functionality of our patients' smiles."

In summary, online advertising through Google Ads and social media is an essential strategy for dental clinics aiming to attract new patients and thrive in a competitive market. By targeting relevant keywords and utilizing demographic targeting, you can ensure your ads reach the right people at the right time. Use Chat GPT to create compelling ads that highlight the benefits of your dental clinic and capture the attention of your target audience. With an effective advertising strategy, you can expand your online presence and attract patients seeking quality dental services.

8. Email and Newsletters for Dental Clinics

Email and newsletters are powerful tools in a dental clinic's marketing arsenal. In this strategy, we will explore how maintaining an email list of patients and sending regular newsletters can strengthen relationships with your patients, keep them informed about their dental health, and attract long-term loyalty. Additionally, we will provide effective strategies for creating and distributing newsletters that generate interest and engagement.

Building an Email List

Before starting to send newsletters, it is crucial to build an email list of patients and individuals interested in your dental clinic. Here are key steps to do so:

1. Request Permission

Always request permission from your patients to add them to your email list. You can do this during their clinic visits or through forms on your website.

2. Offer Incentives

To encourage people to join your list, offer incentives such as a discount on their next dental appointment or the free download of an educational resource on oral health.

3. List Segmentation

Organize your email list into groups based on patients' needs and preferences. This will allow you to send relevant and personalized content.

Creating Effective Newsletters

Once you have a solid list, it's time to create effective newsletters that keep your patients engaged. Here are key steps to follow:

1. Valuable Content

The content of your newsletters should provide value to your patients. Include dental health tips, clinic updates, patient success stories, and special offers.

2. Attractive Design

Use an attractive and clean design for your newsletters. Include high-quality images and ensure they are visually appealing on mobile devices.

3. Consistent Frequency

Maintain a consistent frequency in sending your newsletters, whether it's monthly or quarterly. Consistency helps to keep subscribers engaged.

4. Calls to Action (CTA)

Include clear calls to action in your newsletters. These can be invitations to schedule an appointment, share the newsletter on social media, or take advantage of special offers.

5. Personalization

Use the recipient's name in the greeting and consider personalizing the content based on their needs. This makes the newsletters more relevant.

Newsletter Content Strategies

Below are some effective content strategies for your newsletters:

1. Dental Care Tips

Provide practical dental care tips, such as proper brushing techniques, flossing practices, and selecting oral hygiene products.

2. Patient Success Stories

Share real patient success stories from your clinic. This builds trust and showcases your expertise.

3. Clinic News

Keep patients informed about updates in your clinic, such as the addition of new services, advanced technology, or special events.

4. Special Offers

Provide exclusive discounts on dental treatments and oral care products through your newsletters. This motivates patients to schedule appointments.

Chat GPT Prompt Ideas to Generate Emails with Discounts and Valuable Content

To request ChatGPT to draft an email about discounts on dental and oral health treatments, you can use prompts like:

"Create an email announcing a special 20% discount on dental cleanings and highlight the importance of regular oral hygiene."

"Write an email message offering a 15% discount on teeth whitening and emphasize how a bright smile can boost confidence."

"Generate a promotional email announcing an exclusive discount on orthodontic treatments and explain the benefits of dental alignment."

These prompts can help you create effective email messages that encourage your patients to take advantage of special offers and schedule dental appointments.

9. Free Dental Health Checkup Program

Offering free initial dental check-ups is a powerful strategy that can have a significant impact on your dental clinic. In this strategy, we will explore the importance of implementing a program for free dental health reviews for new patients. You will learn how this initiative not only benefits those seeking dental care but also contributes to building trust and fostering the growth of your clinic.

The Importance of the Initial Dental Check-up

Free initial dental check-ups are an effective way to eliminate barriers that often prevent people from seeking dental care. Many individuals may feel fear, anxiety, or uncertainty before their first appointment with a dentist. Offering free check-ups addresses these issues and provides a range of benefits:

1. Accessibility to Dental Care

Eliminating the initial cost of the consultation makes dental care more accessible for people, especially those without dental insurance or with limited resources.

2. Trust Building

The free initial review is an opportunity to build a trusting relationship with the patient. You can listen to their concerns, answer their questions, and provide them with a positive experience.

3. Education and Prevention

During the review, you can educate patients about the importance of dental prevention. You can provide them with tips on brushing, flossing, and maintaining a healthy diet.

4. Early Detection of Problems

The initial dental review allows for the detection of dental problems at an early stage, making timely and less expensive treatment possible.

Implementation of a Free Review Program

Here are the key steps to implement a free dental health review program in your clinic:

1. Effective Communication

Inform your current patients about the availability of the free review program. Use your website, social media, and clinic staff to promote this offer.

2. Appointment Booking

Make sure to have specific available time slots for the free reviews. This allows for smooth scheduling for interested new patients.

3. Trained Staff

Ensure that your staff is trained to provide a warm and professional welcome to patients arriving for their initial review.

4. Positive Experience

Create a welcoming and pleasant atmosphere in the clinic so that patients feel comfortable and well-cared for during their visit.

5. Continuing Education

During the review, educate patients about the benefits of regular dental care and the prevention of oral problems.

Promotion on Social Networks

Social media is an effective channel to promote your free dental health review program. Here's a prompt idea to ask Chat GPT to draft a Facebook post offering a complimentary dental check-up to followers:

Chat GPT Prompt Ideas for Facebook Post

"Create a Facebook post offering our followers the opportunity to receive a free initial dental check-up at our clinic. Highlight the benefits of this offer, such as early detection of dental problems. Encourage interested individuals to contact us to

schedule their free check-up."

"Write a Facebook post celebrating Dental Health Month. As part of our initiative, we are offering free initial dental check-ups throughout the month. Emphasize for our followers to take advantage of this opportunity to take care of their smiles."

"Craft a Facebook post highlighting the benefits of dental prevention. With our free initial dental check-ups, you can detect and address dental problems before they become major concerns. End with a persuasive call to action for them to contact us and schedule an appointment."

"Create a Facebook post showcasing the value of a healthy smile in everyday life and how it affects confidence and self-esteem. Mention that we offer free initial dental check-ups so they can keep their smiles in their best shape."

"Compose a Facebook post presenting a fun dental health-related contest inviting my followers to participate and win a free initial dental check-up. Ask them to share their best dental care tip in the comments for a chance to win. Ensure to mention that all participants will receive a special discount on their next dental appointment with us."

In summary, a free dental health check-up program is a powerful strategy that benefits both patients and your dental clinic. It removes initial barriers to seeking dental care, establishes trust relationships, and promotes dental prevention. Use social media to promote this offer and attract new patients interested in taking care of their oral health.

10. Automated Customer Service System with Chatbots

In the digital era, customer service is a fundamental aspect of the success of any dental clinic. Patients appreciate efficiency and availability in addressing their questions and concerns. This is where chatbot technology comes into play. In this section, we will explore how an automated customer service system, powered by a chatbot, can revolutionize the way you interact with your patients. You will discover how to use this innovation to respond to frequently asked questions and enhance the overall experience for your patients.

The Power of Chatbots in Customer Service

A chatbot is a computer program designed to interact with users and respond to questions in an automated manner. Integrating chatbots into the customer service of your dental clinic can provide a range of notable benefits:

1. 24/7 Availability

Unlike traditional customer service, chatbots can be available 24 hours a day, 7 days a week. This means that patients can get answers at any time, even outside of business hours.

2. Quick and Accurate Responses.

Chatbots are designed to provide accurate responses instantly. They can answer common questions about schedules, services, treatments, location, and more without delay.

3. Workload Reduction

By handling frequently asked questions and routine tasks, chatbots free up your customer service staff to address more complex issues and provide a more personalized service.

4. Improves the Patient Experience

The ability to get quick and accurate answers contributes to a positive patient experience, increasing satisfaction and loyalty.

Building an Effective Chatbot

Building an effective chatbot requires careful planning and the use of appropriate tools. Here are key steps to create a chatbot that provides an exceptional patient experience:

1. Identify Clear Objectives

Define the goals of your chatbot. What specific questions and tasks should it be able to handle? This will help you design a chatbot that meets the needs of your patients.

2. Design a Natural Conversation

Create a conversation flow that is as natural as possible. The chatbot should be able to understand questions in human language and respond in a comprehensible manner.

3. Solid Knowledge Base

Feed your chatbot with a solid knowledge base that includes information about your services, treatments, hours, and answers to frequently asked questions.

4. Integration with Website and Social Media

Integrate the chatbot into your website and social media profiles so that patients can access it conveniently.

5. Testing and Continuous Improvements

Conduct thorough testing to ensure the chatbot functions correctly. Gather user feedback and make continuous improvements based on their experiences.

Tools to Build a Chatbot

There are numerous tools available to build an effective chatbot for your dental clinic. Here are some popular options:

1. Dialogflow from Google

Dialogflow is a Google-developed chatbot development platform that uses artificial intelligence to create natural conversations. You can design and train your chatbot effectively using this tool.

2. Microsoft Bot Framework

Microsoft Bot Framework is a versatile platform that allows the creation of highly customizable chatbots. It offers integration with Microsoft Azure to harness the power of the cloud.

3. IBM Watson Assistant

IBM's Watson Assistant is a chatbot tool that utilizes IBM's artificial intelligence to provide accurate and personalized responses. It is suitable for high-level enterprise applications.

4. ManyChat

ManyChat is a chatbot creation tool focused on marketing automation on Facebook Messenger. It is user-friendly and suitable for dental clinics looking to engage with patients through this platform.

5. Tars

Tars is a chatbot creation platform that focuses on building high-conversion conversation bots. It is ideal for chatbot implementations on websites and marketing campaigns.

6. ChatRace

ChatRace is a platform that allows you to create chatbots to interact with customers through various messaging channels such as Messenger, WhatsApp, Instagram, and SMS, among others. These chatbots are designed to automate customer support and enhance user experience by providing quick and accurate responses to their questions and inquiries.

Chat GPT Prompt Ideas to Define Interactions for a Chatbot

To start developing effective interactions for your chatbot, here are some prompt ideas:

"Design a chatbot interaction that allows my patients to schedule dental appointments directly from our website."

"Create a conversation flow for a chatbot that answers frequently asked questions about our dental services and operating hours."

"Develop a chatbot interaction that provides information on the importance of oral hygiene and offers dental care tips."

"Give me ideas for a chatbot response to inquiries related to the

location of our dental clinic and directions on how to get there."

These prompts will help you begin designing specific interactions for your chatbot, tailored to the needs of your patients and the information you want to provide.

11. Local Media Advertising for Your Dental Clinic

Local media advertising is a valuable strategy to promote your dental clinic and reach a nearby audience. In this section, we will explore the importance of this strategy and how you can leverage local media resources to increase the visibility of your clinic and attract new patients. Additionally, at the end of the chapter, we will provide Chat GPT prompt ideas to create a community magazine article about the importance of oral health and an offer for a free check-up.

The relevance of local media advertising

Local media advertising offers numerous advantages for your dental clinic. Here are some reasons why this strategy is essential:

1. Community engagement

Advertising in local media connects you directly with the community you serve. You can build strong relationships with your neighbors and establish trust in your clinic.

2. Precise Targeting

Local media allows you to precisely target your audience, reaching people who live or work in the vicinity of your dental clinic. This maximizes the relevance of your advertisements.

3. Increased Visibility

Local media advertising increases the visibility of your dental clinic in the local area. People who see your ads in newspapers, community magazines, or hear them on local radio stations are more likely to remember you when they need dental care.

4. Credibility and Trust

Being present in local media can increase the perception of your clinic as an integral part of the community. This contributes to credibility and patient trust.

Effective Strategies for Local Media Advertising

Here are some effective strategies to implement local media advertising:

1. Local Newspaper Ads

Place ads in local newspapers to promote your dental services and special offers. Ensure that the ads are engaging and contain clear contact information.

2. Community Magazines

Collaborate with community magazines to write informative articles about oral health and the importance of regular dental check-ups. These educational articles will help establish you as an authority in the field.

3. Advertising on Local Radio Stations

Consider the possibility of buying advertising time on local radio stations to broadcast engaging radio ads that reach a wide audience.

4. Sponsorship of Local Events

Sponsor local community events such as fairs, charity runs, or festivals. This allows you to promote your clinic while actively engaging with the community.

5. Advertising in Local Digital Media

Take advantage of advertising opportunities in local digital media, such as local news websites or social media. These channels allow you to reach an online audience in your area.

Ideas for Chat GPT Prompts for a Community Magazine Article

To create a community magazine article about the importance of oral health and offer a free dental checkup, you can use the following Chat GPT prompt ideas:

"Write an [word count] word article emphasizing the importance of oral health in everyday life. Mention the benefits of a healthy smile and how regular dental care can prevent dental problems."

"Craft a brief article for a community magazine promoting oral health. Offer readers a free dental checkup at our clinic as a gesture of care to the community."

"Compose a [word count] word article highlighting the connection between good oral health and overall health. Announce that our clinic offers free dental checkups to promote preventive care."

"Create a 50-word article for a community magazine underscoring the importance of oral health at all ages. Invite readers to take advantage of a free dental checkup at our clinic."

These prompts will help you create a persuasive and educational community magazine article that encourages people to prioritize their oral health and take advantage of the free checkup offer at your dental clinic.

12. Webinars and Educational Videos to Boost Your Dental Clinic

In the digital age, education and access to information are essential for attracting and retaining patients in your dental clinic. Webinars and educational videos are powerful tools that allow you to reach your audience effectively. In this section, we will explore how to organize online webinars and create educational videos related to dental health to promote your clinic and strengthen your relationship with patients. Additionally, at the end of the chapter, we will provide Chat GPT prompt ideas to create an Instagram post advertising a free webinar on oral health.

Online Webinars

Webinars, or web seminars, are online events that allow you to broadcast live or record interactive presentations on topics relevant to your audience, in this case, dental health. Here are some key advantages of hosting webinars.

Real-time connection

Live webinars allow you to interact with your audience in real-time, answer questions, and establish a direct connection.

Global accessibility

You can reach a global audience without geographical limitations, expanding the reach of your dental clinic.

Valuable Content

Providing quality educational content demonstrates your expertise and commitment to dental health.

Hosting Successful Webinars

Here are some key steps to hosting effective webinars:

1. Relevant Topic

Choose a topic of interest for your audience, for example: "How to Maintain a Healthy Smile" or "Common Dental Procedures".

2. Promotion

Promote your webinar on social media, website, and through email. Provide information about the date, time, and how to register.

3. Quality Content

Prepare a high-quality educational presentation and practice before the event to ensure it flows smoothly.

4. Live Interaction

Encourage audience participation with live questions and answers. Respond to participants' questions to create an interactive experience.

5. Recording

Record the webinar for those who cannot attend live and publish it on your website and social media.

Educational Videos

Educational videos are an effective way to present information visually and attractively. They can cover topics such as dental hygiene tips, dental procedures, and patient testimonials. Some advantages of educational videos include:

Visual appeal

Videos are highly visual and can simplify complex concepts in an understandable manner.

Easy to share

Videos can be easily shared on social media and websites, increasing their reach to your audience.

Content Diversity

You can create a variety of videos, from brushing demonstrations to explanations of procedures, to keep your audience engaged.

Creating Impactful Educational Videos

When creating educational videos, consider the following tips:

1. Keep the videos short and focus on a specific topic.

2. Use graphics, animations, or infographics to explain concepts.

3. Include testimonials from satisfied patients.

4. Promote your videos on social media and on your website.

Chat GPT Prompts Ideas to Promote a Free Webinar on Instagram

Below, we provide Chat GPT prompt ideas that suggest a post on Instagram to announce a free webinar on oral health.

"Create an Instagram post announcing our upcoming free webinar on oral health, taking place on [day] of [month] via Instagram Live."

"Describe what photo or illustration I can use in an Instagram

post to promote a free webinar on oral health and home dental care."

"Suggest an image for the Instagram post to promote a webinar on a healthy smile and oral health, and tell me on which stock photo platforms I could find it."

"Draft a short text for my patient email list to promote my webinar about the importance of proper tooth brushing, emphasizing that I am a professional with extensive expertise in the field."

"Write an Instagram post highlighting the exclusive benefits of our free webinar on oral health. Emphasize what participants will learn and how this can improve their dental health and quality of life."

These prompt ideas will help you create a compelling Instagram post that engages your audience and generates interest in your free oral health webinar.

13. Children's Dental Care Program

Children's dental care is crucial to ensure healthy smiles throughout life. In this strategy, we will explore the creation of a specific dental care program for children in your dental clinic. By offering specialized services such as dental exams for young children, dental sealants, and cavity prevention programs, you can attract parents concerned about their children's oral health and provide exceptional care from an early age.

Children's Dental Care Program

Childhood dental care is essential to ensure healthy smiles throughout life. In this strategy, we will explore the creation of a specific dental care program for children in your dental clinic. By offering specialized services such as dental exams for young children, dental sealants, and cavity prevention programs, you can attract parents concerned about their children's oral health and provide exceptional care from an early age.

1. Early Prevention

Detecting and addressing dental issues at early stages can prevent serious complications in the future. Regular dental exams from an early age are crucial.

2. Education and Healthy Habits

Children's dental care provides an opportunity to educate them about the importance of brushing, flossing, and maintaining healthy dental care habits.

3. Confidence and Comfort

By introducing children to the dental environment early on, they become familiar with it and feel more confident in future visits. This reduces anxiety and fear of the dentist.

4. Cavities Prevention

Dental sealants and cavity prevention programs help prevent the formation of cavities, protecting primary and permanent teeth.

Creating a Children's Dental Care Program

1. Dental Exams for Young Children

Initiate dental exams as soon as the child's first teeth erupt. This allows for early detection of issues and guidance on proper oral hygiene.

2. Dental Sealants

Dental sealants are a protective layer applied to the chewing surfaces of molars to prevent the accumulation of plaque and cavities.

3. Cavity Prevention Programs

Implement prevention programs that include education on nutrition, oral hygiene habits, and fluoride to strengthen teeth.

4. Child-Friendly Care

Create a child-friendly dental care environment, with staff trained in child handling and appealing decor for the little ones.

5. Parental Involvement

Encourage parental involvement in their children's dental visits. Educate parents on how to care for their children's oral health at home.

Ideas for Chat GPT Prompts on the Importance of Dental Checkups and Prevention in Children

To promote the importance of dental checkups and disease prevention in children, you can create a blog post. Here are Chat GPT prompt ideas to help you draft this post.

"Write a blog article highlighting the importance of early dental checkups for children. Explore how early detection of dental problems can save smiles. At the end, suggest which photo could accompany this article."

"Create a blog post offering tips to parents on caring for their children's oral health from the first tooth. Emphasize the importance of brushing and flossing."

"Write a blog entry that explains in detail how dental sealants work and why they are beneficial for cavity prevention in children. Provide examples of successful cases. Finally, include a call to action for them to contact the clinic to schedule a checkup."

"Create a blog post that promotes early dental care and provides tips to make dentist visits less stressful for children. Emphasize the importance of a friendly environment. Finally, give a suggestion for which photo could accompany this post."

These prompts will help you create a blog post that informs and educates parents about the importance of dental checkups and disease prevention in children, which can be crucial for attracting more families to your dental clinic.

14. Exceptional Patient Care Program

In the world of healthcare and dentistry, patient care goes beyond clinical skill; it's about providing an exceptional experience. In this strategy, we will explore the importance of an exceptional patient care program in your dental clinic. Training your staff to deliver exceptional customer service not only enhances patient satisfaction but can also lead to positive recommendations and reviews, which are crucial for the continued growth and success of your dental practice.

The Importance of Patient Care

Patient care is not just about treating dental diseases but about taking care of the person as a whole. Here are key reasons why it is fundamental.

1. Patient Satisfaction

A satisfied patient is more likely to return to your clinic and follow your treatment recommendations. Exceptional care fosters satisfaction.

2. Recommendations and Referrals

Happy patients become ambassadors for your clinic. When they experience exceptional care, they are more likely to recommend your services to friends and family.

3.Positive Online Reviews

Positive online reviews are valuable in the digital age. Patients who feel valued and well-cared-for are more likely to leave positive reviews on review sites, such as Google Business Profile.

4. Trust and Loyalty

Exceptional care builds trust. Patients trust your expertise and become loyal to your dental clinic.

Implementing an Exceptional Patient Care Program

1. Staff Training

Train your staff on the importance of patient care. Teach them to actively listen, communicate effectively, and treat each patient with empathy and respect.

2. Clear Communication

Encourage clear and effective communication both in personal interactions and clinical information. Ensure that patients understand their treatments and options.

3. Personalization of Care

Treat each patient individually. Understand their specific needs and concerns to provide personalized care.

4. Dedicated Time

Allocate sufficient time for each appointment to prevent patients from feeling rushed. Personalized care should not feel hurried.

5. Post-Treatment Follow-Up

Follow up with patients after treatments to ensure they are satisfied and to address any concerns they may have.

Chat GPT Prompt Ideas to Promote Friendly and Informative Care

Here are some examples of Chat GPT prompts to help you brainstorm ideas on how to treat your patients in a friendly and informative manner and keep them well-informed.

"Write a welcome message that can be used at the clinic reception to greet patients in a friendly manner and make them feel comfortable from the start."

"Provide an example of how to explain a dental procedure clearly and friendly to a patient who may be anxious. Emphasize the importance of conveying reassurance."

"Write a response for dental clinic staff on how to handle a situation where a patient has additional questions after an appointment. Show empathy and willingness to assist."

"Create a friendly follow-up message for WhatsApp that can be sent to patients after a treatment. Ask how they are feeling and if they have any questions or concerns. Maintain a friendly and amicable tone."

"Help me draft a friendly reminder for my patient, reminding them that their next dental appointment is on [day] of [month] at [time] hrs."

These prompt ideas will help you maintain a friendly and amicable approach to patient care, ensuring that patients feel valued and well-informed at all times. Exceptional patient care is a valuable investment that benefits both your dental practice and the health and satisfaction of your patients.

15. Dental Hygiene Classes

Education on dental hygiene is essential for proper oral care and the prevention of oral diseases. In this section, we will explore the idea of offering free or low-cost dental hygiene classes at your dental clinic. These classes provide an invaluable opportunity to teach patients about proper oral care and encourage prevention. Additionally, at the end of the chapter, we will provide Chat GPT prompt ideas to help you create a Facebook post and promote a free family oral hygiene class.

The Importance of Dental Hygiene Education

Dental hygiene education is crucial for maintaining a healthy smile and preventing oral diseases. Here are some reasons why this education is essential.

1. Disease Prevention

Knowledge about proper brushing, flossing, and maintaining a balanced diet can prevent the formation of cavities, gum diseases, and other dental problems.

2. Healthy Habits

Education promotes the adoption of healthy oral care habits from an early age, which can have a positive impact throughout life.

3. Awareness

Patients should understand the importance of regular dental visits and how to maintain their oral health between appointments.

4. Reducing Dentist Fear

Education can also help reduce fear or anxiety related to dental visits, as patients know what to expect.

Offering Dental Hygiene Classes

1. Theme and Content

Design classes that address relevant topics, such as brushing techniques, proper flossing, choosing oral care products, and the relationship between diet and oral health.

2. Duration and Format

Consider the duration of the classes and the most suitable format. Live online classes, such as those conducted on YouTube or Instagram Live, are effective for reaching a broad audience.

3. Visual Resources

Utilize visual resources, such as graphics and hands-on demonstrations, to make the classes informative and engaging.

4. Interaction

Encourage interaction with participants by answering questions and encouraging active participation.

5. Materials and Samples

Provide sample materials, such as toothbrushes and dental floss, for participants to practice the learned techniques.

Chat GPT Prompt Ideas to Promote Oral Hygiene Classes

Here are some Chat GPT prompt ideas to help you create a Facebook post and promote a free family oral hygiene class that will be conducted live on YouTube.

"Write a Facebook post announcing our exciting family oral hygiene class scheduled for [day] of [month] at [time] hrs. Highlight the importance of maintaining healthy smiles."

"Create a description for the Facebook post detailing the topics to be covered in our oral hygiene class, such as brushing techniques and tips for a radiant smile."

"Develop a script for a 30-minute live session on YouTube where

I will explain the importance of oral hygiene and proper teeth brushing. You can include breaks for viewers to ask questions."

"Draft a Facebook post explaining that I will be hosting a live session on [day] of [month] at [time] hrs, discussing proper teeth brushing and its importance for oral care. Specify that interested individuals should subscribe to the channel, as I will be conducting a giveaway of a dental cleaning kit to viewers who stay until the end."

"Compose a promotional text for my free dental brushing class, emphasizing its importance in preventing future dental diseases. Also, highlight that it is suitable for the whole family."

These prompt ideas will help you effectively promote your free oral hygiene class on Facebook, attracting an audience interested in maintaining healthy smiles and learning proper oral care techniques.

16. Visible Technological Upgrades

In the field of dentistry, technology is advancing at an impressive pace, and staying up-to-date with the latest innovations is essential for providing quality care. In this section, we will explore the importance of showcasing cutting-edge dental technologies used in your dental clinic. Demonstrating your commitment to excellence in care is crucial for attracting and retaining patients. Throughout this chapter, we will highlight how visible technological upgrades can make a difference in the growth of your dental clinic.

Advanced Technology in Dentistry

Technology has revolutionized dentistry in various ways. Here are some cutting-edge technologies you can highlight in your dental clinic:

1. Digital Radiography

Digital radiographs are faster, more efficient, and reduce radiation exposure. You can emphasize how this technology improves diagnostic accuracy.

2. Laser Dentistry

The use of lasers in dental procedures allows for less invasive treatments and faster recovery. Patients will appreciate the convenience and effectiveness of this technology.

3. Intraoral Scanners

Intraoral scanners eliminate the need for uncomfortable impression molds, making procedures more comfortable for patients.

4. Electronic Health Record Systems

Electronic health record management streamlines administration and access to crucial clinical information.

5. Conscious Sedation

Explore how conscious sedation technology ensures a pain-free and less anxiety-inducing experience during procedures.

Advantages of Highlighting Dental Technology

1. Patient Confidence

Patients associate advanced technology with excellence in care. By showcasing your technology, you instill confidence in your clinical capabilities.

2. Precision and Efficiency

Technology enables more precise and efficient procedures, resulting in high-quality outcomes and reduced recovery time.

3. Patient Comfort

Most advanced technologies are less invasive and reduce patient discomfort during treatments.

4. Competitive Differentiation

Highlighting technology sets you apart from the competition and positions you as a leading dental clinic in innovation.

Chat GPT Prompt Ideas on Making Your Dental Technology Visible

Here are alternative Chat GPT prompts that will help you figure out how to showcase the technical and technological qualities of your dental clinic.

"Compose a brief description of how digital radiography enhances the patient experience in our clinic. Emphasize speed and precision."

"Create a message explaining how laser dentistry has transformed the way we perform dental procedures. Highlight the benefits for the patient."

"Provide ideas on how I can make the technology in my dental

clinic visible and how I can leverage it."

"Write a message that highlights how electronic health record management streamlines administration and improves access to patient information."

"Craft a post explaining how our conscious sedation technology ensures a pain-free and less anxiety-inducing experience for our patients during procedures."

These prompts will help you effectively communicate the advantages of dental technology in your clinic and showcase your commitment to excellence in care. Highlighting these visible technological updates can attract patients seeking advanced and high-quality dental care.

17. Flexible Financing Programs

In the field of dentistry, access to quality treatments is essential for maintaining optimal oral health. However, dental treatments can often be expensive, potentially deterring patients from seeking the necessary care. In this section, we will explore the importance of offering flexible financing programs in your dental clinic. These programs, such as installment plans or interest-free financing, make expensive treatments more affordable and accessible to patients. Throughout this chapter, we will examine how to successfully implement a flexible financing plan in your dental clinic.

The Importance of Access to Dental Care

Access to proper dental care is crucial for maintaining good oral health and preventing serious issues. Below are key reasons why access is essential:

1. Prevention of Serious Problems

Regular dental care helps prevent serious issues such as cavities, gum diseases, and tooth loss, ultimately saving money in the long run.

2. Improved Quality of Life

A healthy smile contributes to a person's self-esteem and confidence, enhancing their overall quality of life.

3. Pain and Discomfort Reduction

Accessing dental care in a timely manner allows patients to effectively address pain and discomfort and prevent it from worsening.

Benefits of Flexible Financing Programs

1. Accessibility

Flexible financing programs make dental treatments accessible to a broader range of patients, regardless of their financial resources.

2. Timely Treatment

Patients can receive the necessary treatment immediately, rather than postponing it due to financial concerns.

3. Patient Loyalty

Providing financing options demonstrates concern for the well-being of patients, fostering patient loyalty and satisfaction.

4. Practice Growth

By eliminating financial barriers, you can attract more patients and contribute to the growth of your dental practice.

Implementing Flexible Financing Programs

1. Assessing Patient Needs

Begin by understanding the financial needs of your patients and provide options that align with their circumstances.

2. Clear Communication

Clearly explain financing options to patients, including terms and conditions. Transparency is key.

3. Financial Partnerships

Consider partnering with financial institutions that offer financing programs. This streamlines the process for patients.

4. Program Promotion

Actively promote your flexible financing programs through your website and social media channels.

5.Staff Training

Train your staff so they can answer patient questions and assist in the application process.

Chat GPT Prompt Ideas to Implement a Flexible Financing Plan

Here are alternative prompts for Chat GPT that will help you generate ideas on how to implement a flexible financing plan for your dental clinic:

"Provide ideas on how to design an installment payment plan that is appealing to patients and easy to manage for the clinic. Consider the duration and interest rates."

"Suggest strategies for effectively communicating flexible financing programs to patients. What key messages should be conveyed?"

"Write a list of steps to establish partnerships with financial institutions offering dental financing. How can a beneficial agreement be negotiated?"

"Offer creative ideas for promoting financing programs on social media. What types of content work best?"

"Describe how to train clinic staff to address patient questions and concerns about financing programs. What is the importance of empathy in these interactions?"

These prompts will help you gather valuable insights on successfully implementing a flexible financing plan in your dental clinic. By making treatments more affordable and accessible, you provide your patients with the opportunity to maintain good oral health without financial concerns.

18. Reminder and Follow-Up Program

Consistency in dental care is crucial for maintaining optimal oral health, but patients often forget appointments or neglect follow-ups on their treatments. In this chapter, we will explore the importance of implementing a reminder and follow-up program in your dental clinic. These automated systems for appointments and follow-up assist in keeping patients engaged and returning to the clinic regularly. Throughout this section, we will examine how you can successfully implement a plan for patient reminders and follow-ups.

The need for patient follow-up

Patient follow-up is essential to ensure they receive the ongoing care they need. Here are key reasons why follow-up is crucial:

1. Treatment compliance

Patients often do not fully adhere to treatment plans. Follow-up helps ensure they complete their procedures.

2. Prevention and early detection

Regular follow-up allows for early detection of dental issues and timely treatment, preventing complications.

3. Building Relationships

Follow-up demonstrates continued interest in the patient's

well-being, strengthening the doctor-patient relationship.

4. Increased Patient Retention

Patients who receive reminders and follow-up are more likely to return and continue their care at the same clinic.

Benefits of a Reminder and Follow-Up Program

1. Improved Appointment Compliance

Automated reminders reduce appointment cancellation rates and help maintain fuller schedules.

2. Enhanced Communication

Patients feel valued when they receive personalized reminders and follow-up, improving communication between the clinic and the patient.

3. Problem Prevention

Regular follow-up allows for the early identification of dental issues, preventing the progression of oral diseases.

4. Improves Patient Retention

Patients who experience active follow-up are more likely to stay with the same clinic for years.

Implementing a Reminder and Follow-Up Program

1. Choosing the Right Technology

Select a dental practice management software system that offers automated reminder and follow-up features.

2. Message Personalization

Customize reminder messages to suit the needs and preferences of the patients.

3. Automated Calendars

Utilize automated calendars to schedule appointment reminders and treatment follow-ups.

4. Staff Training

Train clinic staff to use the system and address patient questions regarding reminders.

5. Ongoing Evaluation

Conduct continuous monitoring and evaluation of the program to ensure its effective functioning.

Chat GPT Prompt Ideas for Implementing a Reminder and Follow-Up Plan

Here are some alternative Chat GPT prompts to help you generate ideas on implementing a reminder and follow-up plan for your dental clinic.

"Provide suggestions on how to customize reminder messages for different types of dental appointments, such as routine check-ups and more complex procedures."

"Write a detailed plan for implementing a patient follow-up system, from selecting software to staff training."

"Give examples of how to communicate to patients the importance of regular follow-ups and how it benefits their oral health."

"Describe how clinic staff can address patient questions about reminders and provide assistance in scheduling appointments."

By keeping patients engaged and ensuring they receive necessary care, you contribute to their long-term oral health.

19 Emergency Services

Dental issues can arise at any time, and when they do, patients need immediate and reliable attention. In this strategy, we will explore the importance of promoting your dental clinic's ability to handle dental emergencies. Ensuring that patients know they can turn to your clinic in times of need is not only a valuable service but can also make a difference in oral health and patient satisfaction. Throughout this section, we will review how to successfully implement emergency services in your dental clinic.

The Importance of Emergency Services

Dental emergencies can be distressing and painful for patients. Providing immediate care not only alleviates the patient's suffering but can also prevent serious complications. Here are key reasons why emergency services are essential.

1. Pain Relief

Dental emergencies often come with intense pain. Providing quick relief is crucial for patient comfort.

2. Prevention of Complications

Timely treatment of dental emergencies can prevent the spread of infections or irreversible tooth loss.

3. Patient satisfaction

Your clinic's ability to respond promptly to emergencies demonstrates care and concern for the patient's well-being.

4. Patient loyalty

Patients who receive care in times of need are more likely to remain loyal to your clinic.

Benefits of promoting emergency services

1. Accessibility

Patients should know they can turn to your clinic for emergency care, increasing the accessibility of your practice.

2. Patient Trust

Promoting emergency services builds trust in your clinical capabilities and the availability of your clinic to assist in critical moments.

3. Preventive Care

Patients who seek emergency care at your clinic may be encouraged to seek regular preventive care.

4. Differentiation from the competition

Promoting emergency services sets you apart from the competition and positions your clinic as one that values immediate patient care.

Implementing Emergency Services

1. Clear Communication

Ensure that patients are aware of the procedures to access emergency services and how to contact your clinic outside regular hours.

2. Prepared staff

Train your staff to handle emergency situations and provide effective and compassionate care.

3. Specialized equipment

Make sure your clinic is equipped with the necessary instruments and supplies to address dental emergencies.

4. Extended hours

Consider offering extended hours or emergency services outside of regular business hours.

5. Active Promotion

Actively promote your emergency services through your website and social media.

Chat GPT Prompt Ideas for Implementing Emergency Services

Here are some alternative prompts for Chat GPT to help you generate ideas on how to implement emergency services in a dental clinic.

"Provide suggestions on how to train staff to handle dental emergencies and provide compassionate care in critical moments."

"Write a detailed plan for promoting emergency services on social media and attracting patients who may need immediate attention."

"Suggest strategies to ensure that your clinic is always well-equipped to handle dental emergencies, including purchasing necessary supplies and equipment."

"Provide examples of how to communicate to patients how to access emergency services and what to expect when they arrive at the clinic."

Implementing emergency services in your dental clinic not only benefits your patients in critical moments but also strengthens the reputation and trust in your practice. With proper preparation and active promotion, you can become a reliable resource for emergency dental care in your community.

20. Live Q&A Sessions

Live question and answer sessions have become an invaluable tool for engaging with the audience in real-time and providing relevant information directly. In this strategy, we will explore how to organize interactive web sessions where dentists answer viewers' questions about dental health, procedures, and home care. These sessions not only educate the community but also strengthen the connection with patients. Throughout this chapter, we will discuss how to plan and successfully execute live question and answer sessions in your dental clinic.

The Importance of Live Q&A Sessions

Live question and answer sessions provide a unique opportunity to:

1. Interactive Education

Viewers can ask questions in real-time and receive direct answers from dental health professionals.

2. Building Trust

Live interaction demonstrates transparency and expertise, strengthening patients' trust in your clinic.

3. Community Connection

These sessions foster an online community of informed and engaged patients.

4. Clinic Promotion

They are an opportunity to showcase your services and expertise, positioning you as an authority in the field.

Benefits of Live Q&A Sessions

1. Audience Engagement

Live sessions capture the audience's attention and keep them engaged during the broadcast.

2. Direct Interaction

Viewers can ask specific questions and receive personalized answers.

3. Content Generation

Live sessions can be recorded and used as content on your website and social media.

4. Patient Loyalty

Satisfied patients who participate in live sessions are more likely to remain loyal patients.

Planning Live Q&A Sessions

1. Clear Theme and Objectives

Choose a relevant theme and set clear objectives for the session.

2. Special Guests

Consider inviting other dental health professionals to provide different perspectives.

3. Active Promotion

Announce the session in advance on your social media, website, and email. You can also send messages or posts reminding about the days left until the session.

4. Platform and Technology

Select a reliable live streaming platform and familiarize yourself with its operation.

5. Live Interaction

Encourage the audience to ask questions and respond interactively. Another strategy is to solicit questions in advance or search related sites for common doubts and frequently asked questions.

Chat GPT Prompt Ideas for Planning Live Q&A Sessions

Here are some alternative Chat GPT prompts that can help you generate ideas on planning and implementing live Q&A sessions.

"Provide some tips on selecting engaging and relevant topics for live Q&A sessions in a dental clinic."

"Write a suggested script for promoting a live session on social media and how to keep the audience engaged and attentive during the broadcast."

"Suggest strategies for involving special guests, such as dental specialists, in live sessions to provide additional information to my patients."

"Give examples of how to use recordings of live sessions as marketing content on the clinic's website."

"Describe how to manage live Q&A effectively and maintain a positive and educational atmosphere."

Live Q&A sessions are a powerful tool for educating the audience, building trust, and strengthening the online community. With proper planning and active promotion, you can make the most of this strategy for your dental clinic.

21. Discounts for Family Groups

Offering special discounts for family groups is a smart strategy to encourage dental care for the whole family. In this section, we will explore how you can implement a family group discount system in your dental clinic. This not only promotes oral health across multiple generations but can also be beneficial for your practice. Throughout this section, I will show you how to plan and successfully execute this strategy.

Importance of Family Group Discounts

Dental care is essential for people of all ages, and promoting family care has several benefits:

1. Promotion of Healthy Habits

When family members receive care together, healthy habits are encouraged, fostering a culture of oral care at home.

2. Convenience for Parents

Offering discounts to families makes it more convenient for parents to schedule dental appointments for themselves and their children.

3. Savings for Families

Discounts alleviate the financial burden for families, motivating them to stay current with their dental care.

4. Patient Loyalty

Satisfied families are more likely to remain loyal patients in the long term.

Benefits of Family Group Discounts

1. Attraction of New Patients

Family discounts can attract new families to your clinic.

2. Increased Patient Retention

Families receiving discounts are more likely to remain regular patients.

3. Generation of Referrals

Satisfied patients with discounts are prone to recommending your clinic to other families.

4. Fostering Long-Term Relationships

Dental care is an ongoing need, which can result in long-term relationships with families.

Implementation of Family Group Discounts

1. Determine the Discount Structure

Decide what type of discounts you will offer, whether on specific services or the total cost of treatment.

2. Clear Communication

Ensure that patients are aware of the discounts and how they can take advantage of them.

3. Active Promotion

Promote the discounts on your website and social media..

4. Facilitate Scheduling

Make scheduling appointments for the entire family easy and convenient.

5. Train your staff

Staff should be prepared to answer questions and explain the discounts.

Chat GPT Prompt Ideas to Implement Family Group Discounts

Here are some alternative prompts for Chat GPT that will help you generate ideas on how to implement a family group discount system in a dental clinic:

"Suggest effective strategies for promoting family discounts for my dental clinic on my website and social media."

"Provide examples of how to structure family group discounts that are attractive and financially viable for my dental clinic."

"Describe how I can use email to communicate discounts to families who have been treated at my dental clinic and encourage them to schedule appointments."

"Provide ideas on how to train my staff so they can effectively explain the discounts offered by my dental clinic to interested families."

"Suggest ways to make the experience of families in my dental clinic exceptional, thereby increasing satisfaction and patient retention."

Offering family group discounts is a strategy that benefits both families and your dental clinic. By making dental care more accessible and affordable, you can play a crucial role in the oral health of the entire family while strengthening the patient base of your practice.

22. Teledentistry Services

Teledentistry has become an essential tool to make dental care more accessible and convenient for patients. In this strategy, we will explore how you can implement teledentistry services in your dental clinic. This innovative mode of care not only benefits patients but can also enhance the efficiency and profitability of your practice. Throughout this chapter, we will discuss how to plan and successfully execute teledentistry services.

The Importance of Teledentistry

Teledentistry offers several advantages for both patients and dental healthcare professionals.

1. Accessibility

It allows patients to receive dental care regardless of their geographical location, increasing access to care.

2. Convenience

Teledentistry facilitates appointment scheduling and treatment follow-up, resulting in a more convenient experience for patients.

3. Reduction of Barriers

Eliminate traditional barriers, such as distance or reduced mobility, that might hinder some patients from seeking dental care.

4. Clinical Efficiency

Teledentistry can enhance clinic efficiency by reducing the need for in-person visits for minor consultations.

Benefits of Teledentistry

1. Attraction of New Patients

Offering teledentistry can attract patients seeking convenience and flexibility in care.

2. Increased Patient Retention

Patients who can access teledentistry services are more likely to remain loyal.

3. Market Expansion

You can reach patients who were previously outside your geographical reach.

4. Operational Efficiency

Teledentistry can increase clinical efficiency and reduce waiting times.

Implementation of Teledentistry Services

1. Teledentistry Platform

Select a reliable teledentistry platform that meets security and privacy requirements.

2. Staff Education

Train your staff to use the technology and deliver quality care through teledentistry.

3. Active Promotion

Announce the availability of teledentistry services on your website and social media.

4. Patient Information

Provide patients with clear information on how to access and use teledentistry services.

5. Security and Regulatory Compliance

Ensure compliance with all privacy and data security regulations when offering teledentistry services.

Teledentistry Platforms

Doxy.me

Doxy.me is a telehealth platform designed specifically for healthcare professionals. It provides secure and encrypted video conferencing functionalities, along with options for scheduling appointments and maintaining patient records.

Dentulu

Dentulu is a teledentistry-focused platform that enables dentists to conduct virtual consultations, share images, and provide dental care advice. It also includes scheduling and billing features.

Denteractive

Denteractive is a teledentistry platform that connects patients with dentists in real-time. It offers video consultations, patient follow-up, and a mobile application to facilitate communication.

Zoom for Healthcare

Zoom is a widely used video conferencing platform that offers a specific version for healthcare. It can be an option for virtual consultations, provided appropriate security measures are implemented.

VSee

VSee is a telehealth platform that provides secure video conferencing services, document sharing, and online collaboration. It is used by healthcare professionals across various fields.

Doximity Dialer Video

Doximity is a social network for healthcare professionals that offers a video conferencing feature called "Doximity Dialer Video." It is an option for teledentistry, especially if you are already a member of the network.

Luma Health

Luma Health is a healthcare-focused communication platform that includes teledentistry features. It allows dentists to schedule virtual appointments and communicate with patients efficiently.

Hippo Health

Hippo Health offers teledentistry services through its telemedicine platform. It facilitates communication with patients and enables case tracking.

Teladoc Health

Teladoc Health is an online healthcare platform that includes teledentistry services. It is an option for those seeking a comprehensive solution for virtual care.

Chiron Health

Chiron Health focuses on teledentistry and provides video conferencing and scheduling tools. It also integrates with practice management systems for a more comprehensive experience.

Before choosing a platform, consider your specific needs, patient information security, and ease of use. Additionally, ensure compliance with local and national telehealth and data privacy regulations.

Chat GPT Prompts Ideas to Implement Teledentistry Services

Here are alternative prompts for Chat GPT to help you generate ideas on how to implement an effective teledentistry service in your dental clinic:

"Suggest strategies to promote teledentistry services among current and potential patients, highlighting their advantages."

"Provide examples of how to conduct a successful initial consultation through teledentistry, including recording medical histories and virtual examinations."

"Describe how to address challenges in teledentistry, such as the lack of physical contact, to ensure comprehensive and effective

dental care."

"Suggest ways to maintain patient data confidentiality and security during teledentistry consultations."

"Provide examples of cases where teledentistry can be especially beneficial, such as emergency consultations or orthodontic follow-ups."

Teledentistry is transforming dental care by making it more accessible and convenient for patients. By properly implementing this care modality, you can enhance the patient experience and strengthen your clinic's position in the current dental market.

Farewell

Throughout this book, we have explored a fascinating world where dentistry and marketing converge to drive the success of dental clinics. We have embarked on a journey that has taken us from the fundamentals of dental marketing to the most advanced strategies, even harnessing artificial intelligence to discover new approaches and enhance care and relationships with our patients.

Within these pages, you have discovered how to attract new patients, retain existing ones, and foster strong relationships within the community. We have delved into digital strategies, such as social media marketing, content marketing, and online advertising. Essential aspects of patient care, including service excellence and personalized attention, have also been addressed.

Teledentistry and automation have emerged as revolutionary tools that can take dental care to an entirely new level. Additionally, we have understood the importance of continuous education and adapting to changing trends in the industry.

As you close this book, I encourage you to reflect on the strategies that resonate most with you and your dental clinic. Each of these strategies is a piece of the puzzle that can help you achieve your goals and provide exceptional dental care.

Remember that dental marketing is not just a matter of advertising, but a way to build strong and lasting relationships with your patients. With a constant focus on the quality of care and a commitment to excellence, you are poised to lead your dental clinic toward a bright and successful future.

Harness these strategies, adapt and personalize your approach according to the needs of your clinic, and above all, keep learning and growing in this exciting intersection of dentistry and marketing.

May your dental clinic continue to grow and thrive, and may your patients enjoy healthy smiles for a lifetime!

www.ingramcontent.com/pod-product-compliance
Lightning Source LLC
Chambersburg PA
CBHW071048290526
45795CB00004B/1376